Where Animals Live

The World of Crabs

Text by Jennifer Coldrey

Photographs by
Oxford Scientific Films

Gareth Stevens Publishing
Milwaukee

Where Crabs Live ⬆

Crabs can be found on rocky, muddy, or sandy seashores all over the world.

During daylight, crabs must hide from their enemies. A rocky shore is a good *habitat* for crabs when the tide is out. The rocks form pools. Here, the crabs can live until the tide comes back in.

Many crabs cannot breathe out of water.
They spend most of their lives in the sea.
When the tide goes out, some crabs stay
in rock pools to be near water.

Some crabs live on open, sandy beaches. ⬆
When the tide goes out, they burrow into
the sand. This keeps them wet and safe
from enemies.

Only their eyes and feelers peep out! ⬇

Tropical Land Crabs

On many tropical shores, there are crabs that live mainly on land.

Some land crabs are like these "Sally Lightfoot" crabs. They live on the rocky shore. ↘

Other land crabs are like ↑ this Ghost Crab. They dig large burrows in the sand.

Fiddler crabs are land crabs that burrow in muddy shores and bays. ➡

The Crab's Body ⬆

Most crabs have a wide, flat body. They are covered with a thick, hard shell.

Crabs have five pairs of legs. They are jointed, and they stick out from the sides of the body. The front legs are claws for grasping food.

Crabs have very good eyesight. They have two large eyes on the end of stalks. They also have two pairs of feelers. These are called *antennae*. ➡

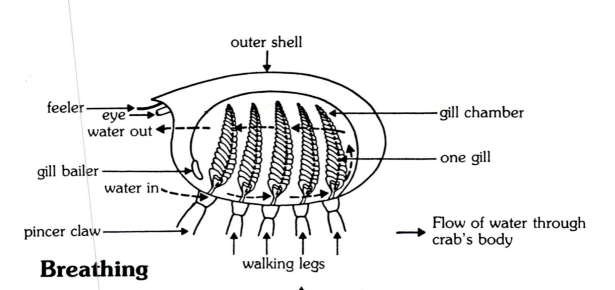

outer shell

feeler

eye

water out

gill bailer

water in

pincer claw

gill chamber

one gill

walking legs

Flow of water through crab's body

Breathing

Crabs breathe like fish.

Oxygen is taken from the water by *gills*. A crab's gills are under its shell on each side of the body.

Crabs have a limb called a gill bailer. It is like a paddle that pushes water into the gill chamber, over the gills, and out through the mouth.

Crabs that burrow draw water into the mouth from above the sand. The water then flows over the gills.

The Masked Crab makes a tube out of its antennae. It then draws water down the antennae and into its mouth.

Land crabs can breathe air. But they must return to the sea to wet their gills.

Molting

Crabs are safe inside their shells. But the shells do not grow. So crabs break their old shells and grow new ones. This is called *molting*.

The new shell is very soft. It takes several days to harden. Until it does, crabs must hide to escape predators that might eat them.

Empty crab shells on the beach make an interesting find! ⬇

Hermit Crabs

Hermit crabs have soft skin. But they do not have hard shells of their own.

←

To protect themselves, they move into empty snail shells.

A hermit crab has two pairs of strong walking legs. It uses them to drag its heavy shell along. ↓

A hermit crab grows and molts inside its shell. Sooner or later, it gets too big for its home. Then it finds a larger shell to move into. First it explores the shell carefully. Then it quickly changes shells!

Movement

Most crabs walk, crawl, or run on their long, jointed legs. They walk sideways or backwards. They almost never walk forwards.

Many crabs cannot swim. They crawl slowly on the bottom of the sea, like this small spider crab. Large crabs cannot chase *prey* that moves quickly. But their hard shells protect them from danger.

Swimming crabs have flat, round back legs, like paddles. These paddles help the crabs swim fast. ⬆

The Ghost Crab is one of the fastest crabs on land. It runs on tip-toe across the beach. ⬇

13

Feeding

Most crabs are *scavengers*. They will eat almost any dead or dying animal — even other crabs!

Some crabs are *predators*. They eat small living animals like worms, fish, or shellfish. ↓

Many crabs have large claws, called pincers, for catching prey.

They break open the hard shells of their prey. Then they scoop out the soft parts.

15

Some crabs don't eat animals. Instead, they feed on seaweed and other plants.

Some crabs, like this fiddler crab, scoop up mud and sand. They then use their mouths to filter off the food.

↑

Some filter-feeders strain tiny food bits from the water.

These crabs strain food with special parts of their mouths. They use these parts like fishnets.

↓

Courtship and Mating

Crabs live separately. But during mating,
the male carries the female with him.
After several days, he fertilizes the eggs
in her body with *sperm*.

The female lays many eggs. She carries
them in a ball beneath her body. A
female carrying eggs is said to be
"in berry."

Land crabs often mate in their burrows, on land. The male attracts the female by dancing. This male fiddler crab also waves his large pincer.

Now and then, the female goes into the water. This is how she keeps her eggs wet. She also returns to the sea to hatch her eggs.

Eggs and Larvae

The female carries her eggs for several weeks or months. She then releases them into the sea. There, they hatch into crab *larvae*.

The larvae float away into the sea. There, they mingle with other tiny plants and animals in the *plankton*.

Two or three weeks after hatching, the larvae begin to look like little crabs. ➡

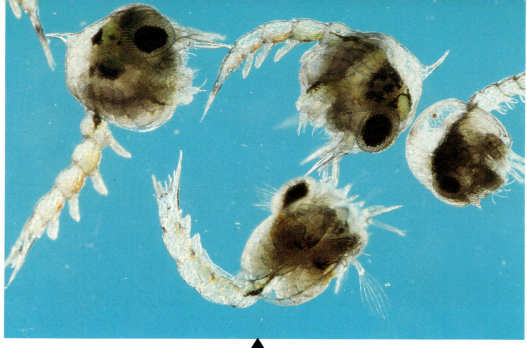

At first, however, the tiny larvae do not look like crabs at all. They have long tails and very large eyes.

Many eggs hatch, but very few survive to become adults.

Predators

Adult crabs have many enemies. On the shore, birds often catch crabs when the tide is out.

Many times the remains of a crab on the beach, ↓

or bird tracks in the sand, will tell a story! ↓

Crabs have many other enemies in the sea. Creatures that eat crabs include other crabs, large fish, squid, and octopuses like this one.

Human Enemies ⬆

To a crab, people are predators, too! We catch crabs in baskets called crab pots. And we use them for food or fish bait.

We also harm all ocean life when we *pollute* the sea. Humans dump chemicals and other poisons into the sea. This kills crabs and the food they need to survive.

Oil spilled at sea is one of the worst kinds of *pollution*. ⬇

Escaping from Danger

Crabs protect themselves in many ways.

Their thick shells cover them like armor.
And their pincers can be used to scare or
even to attack their enemies.

If bothered, some crabs lie completely
still. Others are more brave! They rise up
and wave their pincers in warning.

↑

Some crabs burrow in the sand to escape danger. Or they hide under rocks. Because they are so flat, they can creep into narrow places.

Other crabs cover themselves with seaweed.

↓

Most crabs have good *camouflage*. This makes it hard for predators to see them.

Crabs also have a very strange way of escaping. If one of their legs is caught, it will break off at a special point. Soon, a new leg will grow to replace the old one! This is called *regeneration*.

Neighbors and Partners ↑

Crabs share the seashore with many animals and plants.

We have seen that crabs use some plants, like seaweed, for shelter. Some crabs even use other animals for protection.

This sea anemone has stingers to protect it — and the crab ➡ hiding beneath it!

Hermit crabs sometimes carry sea anemones on their shells. The sea anemone protects the crab. In return, the anemone gets carried to new food supplies. Sometimes the anemone feeds on the crab's leftovers!

↓

Life on the Seashore

On the seashore, crabs are one link in something called the food chain. This means that many plants and animals need each other for food. Here is a drawing that shows which animals eat what.

The Food Chain

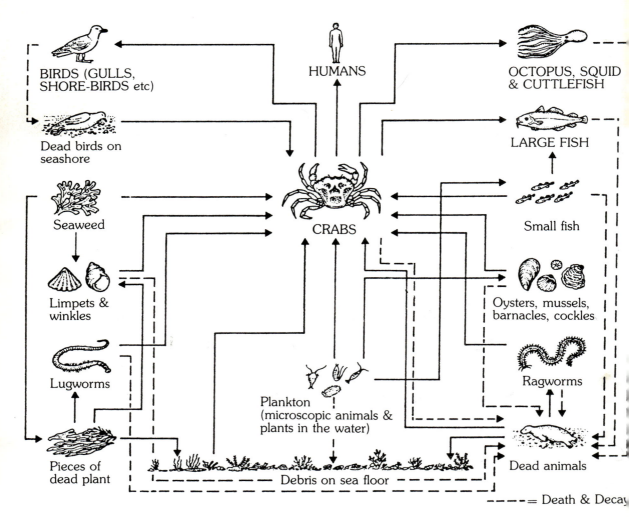

BIRDS (GULLS, SHORE-BIRDS etc)

HUMANS

OCTOPUS, SQUID & CUTTLEFISH

Dead birds on seashore

LARGE FISH

Seaweed

CRABS

Small fish

Limpets & winkles

Oysters, mussels, barnacles, cockles

Lugworms

Ragworms

Plankton (microscopic animals & plants in the water)

Pieces of dead plant

Dead animals

Debris on sea floor

- - - - = Death & Decay

The crab's life is very difficult and dangerous.

The seasons change, and so do the tides. This means that the crab's habitat is also constantly changing. Crabs survive on the seashore because they have adapted to these changes. Their bodies are perfect for their way of life.

New Words About Crabs

These new words about crabs appear in the text in italics, just as they appear here.

antennae . . . . feelers on the crab's head, used for touching, tasting, and smelling.

camouflage . . . . animal disguise; how an animal hides by looking like its surroundings.

gills . . . . special openings on either side of the crab's body, used for breathing (see drawing on page 7).

habitat . . . . the natural home of any plant or animal.

larvae . . . . young forms of certain animals which hatch from the eggs and are totally unlike their parents. A larva has to change its body several times before it becomes an adult.

molting . . . . shedding an old skin or shell.

oxygen . . . . a colorless, odorless, tasteless part of air that dissolves in water; all plants and animals need it to stay alive.

plankton . . . . small animals and plants which float and drift on the sea.

pollute . . . . to make dirty and therefore damage and spoil.

pollution . . . . damage caused to plants, animals, and places, from dirt, rubbish, and poisons left by people.

predators . . . . animals that kill and eat other animals.

prey . . . . animal that is hunted and killed by another animal for food.

regeneration . . . . growing new parts of the body to replace lost or damaged parts.

scavengers . . . . animals that feed on the dead or dying remains of other animals.

sperm . . . . a liquid from male crabs that makes crab eggs grow.

Reading level analysis: SPACHE 2.6, FRY 1, FLESCH 101 (very easy),
RAYGOR 3, FOG 3, SMOG 3

Library of Congress Cataloging-in-Publication Data

Coldrey, Jennifer.
  The world of crabs.

  (Where animals live)
  Summary: Simple text and photographs depict crabs feeding, breeding, and defending themselves in their natural habitats.
  1. Crabs — Juvenile literature. [1. Crabs] I. Oxford Scientific Films. II. Title. III. Series.
  QL444.M33C65 1986   595.3'842   85-30294
ISBN 1-55532-088-0
ISBN 1-55532-063-5 (lib. bdg.)

This North American edition first published in 1986 by
Gareth Stevens, Inc.
7221 West Green Tree Road   Milwaukee, Wisconsin 53223, USA

U.S. edition, this format, copyright © 1986 by Belitha Press Ltd.
Text copyright © 1986 by Gareth Stevens, Inc.
Photographs copyright © 1986 by Oxford Scientific Films.

First conceived, designed, and produced by Belitha Press Ltd., London, as *The Crab on the Seashore*, with an original text copyright by Oxford Scientific Films. Format copyright by Belitha Press Ltd.

Typeset by Ries Graphics ltd.
Printed in Hong Kong
U.S. Editors: MaryLee Knowlton and Mark J. Sachner
Design: Treld Bicknell
Line Drawings: Lorna Turpin
Scientific Consultants: Gwynne Vevers and David Saintsing

The publishers wish to thank the following for permission to reproduce copyright material: **Oxford Scientific Films Ltd.** for pages 1, 2 *below*, 3 *below*, 4 *above* and *below*, 6, 7, 8 *above* and *below*, 10 *above* and *below*, 11, 12 *above* and *below*, 13 *above*, 14 *above* and *below*, 15 *above*, *below middle* and *right*, 17 *above*, 18, 22 *below right*, 23, 25, 26 *above*, 27, 28 *above* and *below* and 29 (photographer G. I. Bernard), pages 2 *above*, 5 *above right*, and 13 *below* (photographer David Thompson), page 3 *above* (photographer Barrie E. Watts), pages 5 *above left*, 9, 21 *above* and *below* and 22 *below left* (photographer Peter Parks), pages 5 *below*, 16 *below*, 26 and 31 (photographer J. A. L. Cooke), page 16 *above* (photographer Godfrey Merlen), page 17 *below* (photographer Rudie H. Kuiter), page 19 (photographer P. & W. Ward), page 20 (photographer Waina Cheng), page 22 *above* (photographer Ronald Templeton), page 24 *above* (photographer R. P. Coldrey), and page 24 *below* (photographer C. M. Perrins).

Front and back cover photographer: G. I. Bernard.